UNLOCKING THE SOUL

UNLOCKING THE SOUL

MOHAMMED ABDUL

First Printing, 2025

Contents

1

Introduction to Memory and the Soul

Understanding Memory and Repression

Understanding memory involves delving into the complex interplay between conscious awareness and the subconscious mind. Memory is not merely a repository of past experiences; it shapes our identity, influences our emotions, and informs our spiritual beliefs. For those who embrace concepts such as reincarnation and spiritualism, the significance of memory extends beyond this lifetime. Repressed memories, often tucked away in the recesses of the mind, can hold keys to understanding previous existences and uncovering profound truths about the soul's journey. Recognizing the nature of memory and the mechanisms of repression is crucial for anyone seeking to unlock these hidden experiences.

Repression acts as a protective mechanism, shielding individuals from painful or traumatic memories that may be too difficult to confront. This psychological phenomenon can obscure valuable insights that lie within repressed experiences. For spiritual seekers, accessing these memories can illuminate patterns of behavior, resolve emotional conflicts, and foster a deeper connection to the soul's purpose. Techniques targeting memory recall, particularly those tailored to past life exploration, can aid in bringing these suppressed memories to the surface, allowing for healing and understanding.

Guided visualization serves as a powerful tool for memory recall, particularly in the realm of past life experiences. By creating a safe and supportive mental space, practitioners can facilitate journeys into previous existences, helping individuals reconnect with memories that may have been long buried. This technique often involves vivid imagery and sensory engagement, enabling deeper access to the subconscious. Coupled with journaling practices, participants can document their experiences, providing a tangible account of their journeys and insights, which can further enhance memory retrieval and integration.

Meditation techniques play an essential role in accessing repressed memories, fostering a calm and receptive state of mind conducive to exploration. Through focused breathwork and mindfulness practices, individuals can quiet the mental chatter that often obscures deeper recollections. Such techniques can lead to transformative experiences, unearthing memories that offer clarity and healing. Additionally, hypnotherapy stands out as a method that can guide individuals safely into their subconscious, often uncovering past life memories and facilitating significant breakthroughs.

Art therapy and breathwork are complementary approaches that encourage the expression and activation of repressed memories. Artistic expression allows individuals to externalize their inner experiences, often revealing insights that may not surface through traditional verbal communication. Similarly, breathwork techniques can enhance emotional release and facilitate deeper connections to memory. When combined with group workshops and shared memory exploration, these practices create a communal space for healing and discovery, fostering a supportive environment where individuals can collectively navigate their journeys through the intricate landscape of memory and repression.

The Connection between Memory and Past Lives

The exploration of memory in relation to past lives presents a fascinating intersection for those who believe in reincarnation and the continuity of the soul. Memory is not merely a repository of past experiences; it is a dynamic entity that can transcend time and space, offering glimpses into previous existences. For spiritualists, understanding how memory functions in this context can enhance their journey of self-discovery and healing. Techniques such as guided visualization and meditation serve as powerful tools, allowing individuals to tap into the depths of their consciousness and access memories that may have remained hidden for years, if not lifetimes.

Guided visualization, in particular, is an effective method for facilitating past life recall. Practitioners often create a safe and inviting mental environment, enabling participants to explore their inner landscapes without fear or resistance. Through this process, memories of past lives can surface, often revealing significant insights about current life challenges and patterns. This technique emphasizes the importance of a relaxed state of mind, which can be achieved through meditation and breathwork, both of which help to quiet the ego and open pathways to deeper memory retrieval.

Journaling practices further enrich the connection between memory and past lives. By documenting thoughts and feelings that arise during meditative states or after guided visualizations, individuals create a tangible record of their experiences. This written account serves not only as a reflective tool but also as a means to identify recurring themes and symbols that may indicate unresolved issues from past lives. As memory retrieval unfolds through these writings, practitioners can begin to weave together a narrative that offers clarity and understanding of their soul's journey across time.

Hypnotherapy stands out as a powerful avenue for accessing past life memories. By inducing a trance state, skilled hypnotherapists can facilitate profound access to the subconscious mind, where repressed memories may reside. This technique often brings forth vivid recollections and emotional releases that can lead to significant healing. Participants frequently report a sense of liberation from fears, phobias, or emotional blockages that have roots in previous incarnations, thereby reinforcing the idea that memory is not just a linear archive but a complex tapestry of experiences that informs the present.

Art therapy also plays a crucial role in exploring repressed experiences linked to past lives. The creative process allows individuals to express emotions and memories that may be difficult to articulate verbally. Through painting, drawing, or other artistic mediums, practitioners can access deeper layers of their subconscious, revealing insights about their past lives. Group workshops and shared memory exploration further enhance this journey, as participants can connect with others who share similar experiences, fostering a sense of community and collective healing. Ultimately, the connection between memory and past lives invites believers to embrace their spiritual journeys with an open heart and a willingness to explore the depths of their souls.

The Importance of Recalling Repressed Experiences

Repressed experiences often serve as barriers to a deeper understanding of the self, particularly for those who resonate with spiritual beliefs such as reincarnation and past life exploration. Engaging with these hidden memories can lead to profound insights, healing, and personal growth. By recalling repressed experiences, individuals can confront unresolved emotions, integrate lessons from past lives, and cultivate a more authentic existence. This process not only enhances spiritual awareness but also promotes emotional well-being, allowing individuals to shed the burdens of unprocessed trauma.

Memory recall is essential for uncovering the layers of the soul's journey through various lifetimes. Techniques such as guided visualization can facilitate this process by creating a safe mental space where individuals can explore their subconscious. During these sessions, practitioners can access memories that may have been buried due to fear or trauma. By visualizing past life scenarios, individuals gain clarity on their current life challenges and patterns, ultimately leading to a transformative healing experience. This method aligns well with the beliefs of spiritualists and believers in reincarnation, who often seek to understand their soul's purpose across different incarnations.

Journaling serves as another powerful tool for memory retrieval, providing a tangible outlet for emotions and thoughts related to repressed experiences. By documenting dreams, intuitive insights, and even spontaneous recollections, individuals can begin to piece together fragmented memories. This practice not only fosters self-reflection but also enhances one's ability to recognize recurring themes from past lives. Incorporating journaling into daily routines encourages a deeper connection with the self, allowing for the exploration of hidden aspects of one's identity that may inform current life experiences.

Meditation techniques, including breathwork and mindfulness practices, are invaluable for accessing repressed memories. These methods promote a calm, centered state that allows individuals to delve deeper into their psyche. Breathwork, in particular, can activate memory recall by enhancing oxygen flow to the brain and facilitating emotional release. As individuals enter a meditative state, they may encounter vivid images or sensations related to past lives, providing critical insights into their spiritual journey. The synergy between meditation and memory activation creates a fertile ground for healing and self-discovery.

Participating in group workshops or utilizing modalities such as hypnotherapy and art therapy can further enrich the journey of memory exploration. These collaborative environments foster a sense of community and shared experience, encouraging participants to unveil their stories within a supportive framework. Techniques like neuro-linguistic programming (NLP) offer structured approaches to enhance memory recall, while dream analysis can illuminate subconscious messages tied to past life experiences. By embracing a multifaceted approach to recalling repressed experiences, individuals can unlock the wisdom of their souls, paving the way for a more enlightened path forward.

2

Memory Recall Techniques for Repressed Experiences

Overview of Memory Recall Techniques

Memory recall techniques offer a diverse range of methods aimed at unveiling repressed experiences, particularly for individuals interested in the exploration of past lives and spiritual dimensions. These techniques are rooted in the understanding that memories, whether from this life or previous incarnations, can be obscured by emotional or psychological barriers. To facilitate the retrieval of these memories, practitioners often employ guided visualization, which encourages individuals to enter a relaxed state where they can visualize past experiences. This method not only enhances memory recall but also allows for a deeper connection with one's spiritual journey, enabling believers in reincarnation to access insights that may have been long forgotten.

Meditation techniques play a crucial role in memory recall, providing a means to quiet the mind and open oneself to deeper layers of consciousness. Through focused breathing and mindfulness, practitioners can enter altered states of awareness that facilitate the emergence of repressed memories. This approach is particularly beneficial for those seeking to explore their past lives, as it fosters an environment where insights can surface naturally. Additionally, breathwork serves as a powerful tool for memory activation, allowing individuals to harness the energy of their breath to unlock memories stored within the body. This somatic experience can reveal not only past life memories but also emotional patterns that influence present behavior.

Journaling practices offer another effective strategy for memory retrieval, enabling individuals to document their thoughts and feelings related to their spiritual experiences. Writing serves as a cathartic outlet, providing a tangible means to explore the intricacies of one's past. This practice can be enhanced through prompts that encourage reflection on dreams, feelings of déjà vu, or specific life events that may connect to prior existences. Moreover, dream analysis can reveal profound insights into past life experiences, as dreams often carry symbolic representations of unresolved issues or lessons from previous incarnations. By examining these dreams, individuals can gain clarity and guidance on their spiritual paths.

Hypnotherapy stands out as a potent method for accessing past lives, as skilled practitioners can guide individuals into deep states of relaxation where memories are more readily accessible. This technique often reveals detailed narratives from previous lives, allowing for profound healing and understanding. Art therapy complements these memory recall techniques by providing a creative outlet for individuals to express and explore their repressed experiences. By engaging in artistic creation, individuals can tap into their subconscious mind, unveiling emotions and memories that may be difficult to articulate verbally.

Finally, group workshops offer a supportive environment for shared memory exploration, enabling participants to engage in collective experiences that foster connection and understanding. These workshops often incorporate various techniques, including neuro-linguistic programming (NLP) to enhance memory retention and spiritual practices to uncover hidden memories. By working together, participants can share insights and validate one another's experiences, creating a rich tapestry of understanding that deepens their spiritual journeys. As believers in reincarnation and spiritual exploration engage with these memory recall techniques, they unlock pathways to understanding their souls' journeys across time, illuminating the profound connections between past and present.

Identifying Repressed Memories

Identifying repressed memories is a nuanced process that requires sensitivity and understanding of the intricate relationship between the mind, spirit, and past experiences. For believers in reincarnation and spiritual practices, recognizing these memories can open pathways to profound insights and personal growth. The journey begins with an awareness that memories may not always be readily accessible; they can be buried deep within the subconscious, often as a protective mechanism against trauma or distressing experiences. It is essential to approach this exploration with compassion and a readiness to confront what may arise.

Guided visualization serves as a powerful tool in the quest to uncover repressed memories. This technique involves entering a meditative state where participants can envision themselves in specific scenarios, often related to past experiences or lifetimes. By creating a safe mental space, individuals can access emotions and images that may have been obscured. It is crucial to set an intention before beginning the visualization, as this focus can help direct the subconscious and facilitate the retrieval of relevant memories. Practitioners often report that this method leads to significant emotional release and clarity about their past.

Journaling practices are another effective means of identifying repressed memories. Writing allows individuals to express thoughts and feelings that may be difficult to articulate verbally. By maintaining a daily journal focused on reflections, dreams, and spontaneous thoughts, one can uncover patterns or recurring themes that point to hidden experiences. This process can be enhanced by prompting questions that encourage deeper introspection, such as "What memories arise when I think of certain places or people?" or "How do my dreams connect to my waking life?" Over time, these reflections can illuminate aspects of one's past that have been forgotten or suppressed.

Meditation techniques also play a vital role in accessing repressed memories. Through mindfulness and focused breathing, individuals can quiet their minds and create a conducive environment for memory recall. Many find that guided meditations specifically designed for exploring past lives or repressed experiences can facilitate breakthroughs in memory retrieval. Regular practice not only enhances awareness of one's mental landscape but also helps to cultivate a deeper connection to the self, making it easier to confront and integrate previously hidden memories.

Finally, group workshops provide a communal space for shared memory exploration, enabling participants to engage in collective healing and insight. This setting fosters a sense of safety and support, encouraging individuals to share their experiences and listen to others. Often, hearing the stories of fellow participants can trigger personal memories and realizations. Additionally, integrating techniques such as art therapy and breathwork within these workshops can enrich the experience, allowing for a multi-faceted approach to uncovering repressed memories. By utilizing these diverse memory recall techniques, individuals can embark on a transformative journey towards understanding their past and unlocking the potential of their soul.

Techniques for Accessing Repressed Memories

Techniques for accessing repressed memories are crucial for individuals seeking to unlock the depths of their consciousness, particularly for those who believe in reincarnation, spiritual phenomena, or have experienced alien abductions. Each method offers a unique pathway to uncover hidden aspects of one's past, facilitating both personal growth and spiritual development. It is essential to approach these techniques with an open mind, allowing for the exploration of memories that may have been buried due to trauma or other significant life events.

Guided visualization stands out as one of the most effective techniques for recalling past life experiences. This method involves a structured journey led by a facilitator or through recorded audio that guides participants into a deep state of relaxation. As individuals visualize their past, they may encounter vivid images, emotions, and sensations that connect them to previous existences. The practice enhances the likelihood of memory retrieval by creating a safe space where the subconscious can reveal its secrets without the interference of conscious judgment.

Journaling practices also play a significant role in memory retrieval. By engaging in regular writing sessions, individuals can tap into their thoughts and feelings, often uncovering memories that have remained dormant. Free writing, in particular, allows for an unfiltered flow of ideas, which can lead to unexpected insights about past lives or repressed experiences. This technique encourages self-reflection and helps articulate the nuances of one's spiritual journey, fostering a deeper understanding of personal narratives that may have been overlooked.

Meditation techniques tailored for accessing repressed memories can enhance the clarity and depth of one's inner exploration. Practices such as mindfulness meditation or transcendental meditation create a mental environment conducive to memory activation. By focusing inward and silencing external distractions, individuals can connect with their inner selves, potentially surfacing memories that have long been obscured. Regular meditation not only aids in memory recall but also cultivates a sense of peace and awareness, which can be integral to the healing process.

Hypnotherapy is another powerful approach for accessing past lives and repressed memories. This technique involves a trained hypnotherapist guiding individuals into a trance-like state where they can explore their subconscious. Under hypnosis, the barriers preventing access to certain memories can dissolve, allowing for profound revelations and emotional releases. Combining hypnotherapy with other modalities, such as art therapy or breathwork, can amplify the memory recall process, enriching the experience and facilitating a more comprehensive exploration of one's soul journey.

3

Guided Visualization for Past Life Recall

The Power of Visualization

The concept of visualization transcends the mere act of imagining; it serves as a profound tool for accessing layers of consciousness that house our repressed and past life memories. For individuals who resonate with the beliefs of reincarnation and spiritual exploration, visualization acts as a bridge to unlock the soul's history, facilitating experiences that may otherwise remain obscured. By harnessing the power of the mind's eye, practitioners can delve into the depths of their psyche, encountering memories that inform their current realities and spiritual journeys.

Guided visualization is particularly effective for those seeking to recall past lives. This technique involves directed imagery, often led by a facilitator, that encourages participants to envision scenes, feelings, and sensations associated with their previous incarnations. As individuals engage in this immersive process, they may find themselves transported to different epochs and environments, revealing insights and lessons pertinent to their present lives. This method not only stimulates memory recall but also fosters a deeper connection to one's spiritual lineage, reinforcing the belief in continuous existence beyond the physical realm.

Journaling practices complement visualization by providing a tangible outlet for the experiences and insights gained during sessions. Writing serves as a means to document memories and emotions that surface, allowing individuals to process their experiences in a structured way. Through reflective journaling, participants can identify patterns, themes, and connections between past lives and their current circumstances. This practice can enhance the clarity of visualization exercises, as the act of writing solidifies memories, making them more accessible for future exploration.

Meditation techniques also play a critical role in enhancing the effectiveness of visualization for memory recall. By calming the mind and centering the spirit, meditation creates a fertile ground for deeper introspection. During meditation, individuals can visualize specific scenarios or past life experiences, tapping into intuitive insights that may arise from the subconscious. The stillness achieved through meditation allows for a clearer connection to higher consciousness and the exploration of repressed memories, facilitating a richer understanding of one's journey across time.

The integration of various modalities, such as hypnotherapy, art therapy, and breathwork, further enriches the practice of visualization. Hypnotherapy can induce a trance-like state where individuals are more susceptible to recall memories hidden in their subconscious. Art therapy provides a creative outlet to express and explore emotional responses to these memories. Meanwhile, breathwork techniques can activate dormant memories by enhancing consciousness and awareness. Collectively, these practices create a holistic approach to memory retrieval, empowering believers in reincarnation and spiritualism to uncover the profound truths of their existence.

Steps for Effective Guided Visualization

Guided visualization is a powerful tool for those seeking to explore their past lives and unlock repressed memories. The process begins with creating a serene environment that encourages relaxation and openness. Choose a quiet space free from distractions, where you feel safe and comfortable. Dim the lights or use soft lighting, and consider incorporating elements that evoke a sense of peace, such as gentle music, incense, or essential oils. This environment sets the stage for a deeper connection with your inner self and facilitates the visualization process.

The next step involves centering your mind and body through meditation. Begin by focusing on your breath, inhaling deeply and exhaling slowly. This practice not only calms the nervous system but also enhances your ability to tune into your subconscious mind. As you settle into a meditative state, visualize a warm, protective light surrounding you. This light acts as a shield against negative energies, allowing you to delve deeper into your memories without fear or hesitation.

Once you feel grounded and secure, initiate the guided visualization by envisioning a serene landscape that resonates with you. This could be a tranquil forest, a peaceful beach, or a sacred space. Allow yourself to explore this landscape freely, noticing the sights, sounds, and sensations around you. As you wander, invite any past life memories to surface organically. You may encounter symbols, figures, or emotions that are significant to your journey. Trust the process, and do not force any images or memories; rather, allow them to come to you naturally.

As memories begin to unfold, it is essential to document your experiences. Keep a journal handy to jot down any insights, images, or feelings that arise during and after your visualization. This practice not only reinforces your recall but also aids in processing the memories you access. Reflecting on your experiences through writing can reveal patterns or themes that may require further exploration, enhancing your understanding of your past lives and their relevance to your current existence.

Finally, consider integrating additional techniques such as breathwork or artistic expression to deepen your exploration. Breathwork can help activate memories and emotions, while art therapy allows for a non-verbal expression of your experiences. Engaging in group workshops or discussions with like-minded individuals can also provide valuable insights and support. This multifaceted approach to guided visualization ensures a comprehensive journey into your past, fostering greater self-awareness and spiritual growth.

Case Studies in Past Life Recall

Case studies in past life recall provide compelling evidence of the potential for individuals to access memories from previous incarnations. These accounts often illustrate the profound impact that such memories can have on a person's understanding of their current life, relationships, and spiritual journey. Through various memory recall techniques, individuals have reported experiences that transcend the boundaries of conventional understanding, revealing insights into their soul's journey across time.

One notable case involved a woman named Sarah, who, during a guided visualization session, vividly recalled a life as a healer in a small village during the 18th century. As she delved deeper into the visualization, she experienced emotions and sensory details that felt overwhelmingly real. This experience not only allowed her to explore her passion for healing in her current life but also provided clarity about her fears related to medical practices, stemming from her past life experiences. The insights gained from this session led her to pursue integrative healing methods, reinforcing her belief in the interconnectedness of past and present.

Another intriguing example comes from a series of group workshops focused on shared memory exploration, where participants utilized breathwork and guided meditation to access suppressed memories. In one session, a participant named David discovered that he had lived as a sailor during a time of exploration and conflict. The memories revealed profound themes of courage and adventure, which resonated with his current life challenges. This exploration not only fostered personal growth but also cultivated a sense of community among participants, as they shared their findings and supported each other in their journeys of discovery.

Art therapy has also emerged as a powerful tool for exploring repressed experiences, particularly in accessing past life memories. In one case, an artist named Maria began creating visual depictions of her dreams, which led her to uncover memories of a past life as a painter in Renaissance Italy. Her artwork became a conduit for expressing emotions and experiences that had long been buried. As she analyzed her creations, Maria recognized patterns and symbols that aligned with her current life's challenges, allowing her to process and integrate these experiences in a therapeutic manner.

Finally, hypnotherapy has been instrumental in facilitating past life recall for many individuals seeking to understand their soul's evolution. A case study involving a client named Tom highlighted the effectiveness of hypnotic regression in unveiling memories of a previous life as a soldier. Through guided sessions, Tom confronted feelings of guilt and unresolved trauma, ultimately leading to significant healing. His journey emphasized the importance of addressing past life experiences to foster emotional well-being in the present. These case studies collectively underscore the transformative potential of memory recall techniques, offering believers in reincarnation and spiritual seekers pathways to uncover hidden memories and enhance their understanding of the soul's journey.

4

Journaling Practices for Memory Retrieval

The Role of Journaling in Memory Retrieval

Journaling serves as a powerful tool for memory retrieval, particularly for those who seek to access repressed and past life memories. Writing down thoughts and experiences can help individuals process complex emotions and uncover hidden fragments of their past. For believers in reincarnation and spiritual exploration, journaling provides a safe space to articulate feelings and insights that may arise during meditation, guided visualization, or hypnotherapy sessions. This act of writing not only organizes thoughts but also creates a tangible record that can be revisited, allowing for deeper reflection and understanding over time.

Engaging in regular journaling practices encourages a dialogue with the subconscious mind. When individuals write freely, they may tap into memories that have been suppressed or overlooked. This process can be particularly beneficial for those who have experienced alien abductions or other extraordinary events, as the act of documenting these experiences can lead to greater clarity and insight. By allowing thoughts to flow onto the page without judgment, individuals often find that they encounter memories that feel familiar yet elusive, making journaling an essential practice for memory recall.

In addition to serving as a personal record, journaling can enhance other memory retrieval techniques such as meditation and guided visualization. After engaging in these practices, individuals can write about their experiences, capturing the emotions and imagery that surfaced. This not only reinforces the memories but also facilitates a deeper understanding of their significance. By reflecting on these entries, practitioners can identify patterns and themes that emerge, which may provide clues to their past lives or repressed experiences that need to be addressed.

Art therapy and journaling can intersect beautifully, allowing individuals to express their memories in both written and visual forms. Creating art alongside writing can unlock deeper layers of memory, as artistic expression often bypasses the analytical mind. This holistic approach supports the retrieval process by integrating various modalities of self-expression, enabling a richer exploration of past lives and repressed experiences. The synergy between art and journaling cultivates a deeper connection to the self, enhancing the overall memory retrieval experience.

Ultimately, journaling is not merely a solitary endeavor; it can also be a shared practice within group workshops focused on memory exploration. Participants can exchange insights and experiences, enriching their understanding of their own memories while supporting one another in their journeys. The collective energy of a group can amplify individual experiences, paving the way for profound revelations. By incorporating journaling into their spiritual practices, believers in reincarnation and memory retrieval can unlock the potential for healing and self-discovery, fostering a deeper connection to their past and the mysteries of their existence.

Techniques for Effective Journaling

Journaling serves as a powerful tool for individuals seeking to unlock their memories, especially for those engaged in the exploration of past lives and repressed experiences. The act of writing not only facilitates memory retrieval but also provides a safe space for reflection and emotional release. To embark on this journey, it is essential to cultivate a practice that encourages openness and curiosity. This includes setting aside dedicated time for journaling, creating a tranquil environment, and approaching the process with a mindset of exploration rather than judgment.

One effective technique is free writing, which involves setting a timer and writing continuously without self-editing or pausing to reflect. This unfiltered approach allows thoughts and memories to flow freely onto the page, often revealing insights that might remain hidden through structured writing. To enhance this practice, individuals can incorporate prompts related to their spiritual beliefs, such as questions about past lives or experiences of alien encounters. This targeted focus can help trigger memories that are deeply buried, allowing for a richer exploration of the self.

Incorporating guided visualization into the journaling process can also prove beneficial. Before beginning to write, practitioners can engage in a short visualization exercise aimed at connecting with their inner selves or specific past life experiences. This might involve imagining a serene landscape or a significant moment from a past existence. After this visualization, individuals can journal about the imagery and feelings that emerged, providing a deeper understanding of their memories and emotions. These guided sessions can foster a stronger connection to one's intuition and enhance the overall journaling experience.

Additionally, the integration of art therapy into journaling practices can facilitate the exploration of repressed memories. Rather than relying solely on words, individuals can express their thoughts and feelings through drawings or collages that represent their experiences. This creative outlet can often bypass the conscious mind, allowing for a more profound exploration of hidden memories. Following the artistic expression, individuals can write about their creations, examining what the imagery reveals about their past lives or spiritual experiences.

Lastly, establishing a routine that includes meditative practices before journaling can significantly enhance memory recall. Meditation quiets the mind and opens pathways to deeper consciousness, making it easier to access repressed memories. By combining these techniques—free writing, guided visualization, art therapy, and meditation—individuals can create a holistic journaling practice that not only aids in memory retrieval but also fosters spiritual growth and self-discovery. In doing so, they will be better equipped to unlock the mysteries of their soul's journey across time and space.

Analyzing Journal Entries for Insights

Analyzing journal entries can serve as a powerful gateway to unlocking repressed experiences and gaining insights into past lives. For believers in reincarnation and spiritualism, the written word often captures fleeting memories and emotions that may otherwise remain obscured. By meticulously documenting thoughts, feelings, and dreams, individuals create a rich tapestry of their inner worlds, which can be revisited and analyzed for deeper understanding. This process not only aids in memory retrieval but also encourages a dialogue between the conscious and subconscious mind, allowing for the emergence of insights that may have been buried over time.

When delving into journal entries, it is essential to approach the material with an open and curious mindset. Each entry represents a snapshot of consciousness, reflecting the individual's state of being at that moment. As you read through past writings, pay attention to recurring themes, symbols, and emotions. These elements often signify unresolved issues or significant past life connections. Engaging in this reflective practice can illuminate patterns that may suggest the presence of repressed memories, guiding you toward further exploration through techniques such as guided visualization or meditation.

Incorporating art therapy into the analysis of journal entries can enhance the understanding of repressed experiences. Visual representations of feelings or memories can emerge when words fail to encapsulate the depth of an experience. Create visual prompts based on journal entries and observe how they resonate with your emotional landscape. This method creates a multi-dimensional view of your memories, enabling you to explore aspects of your existence that may relate to past life experiences. Art can act as a catalyst, facilitating a deeper connection with your inner self, and revealing insights that might otherwise remain hidden.

Breathwork and neuro-linguistic programming can further augment the analysis of journal entries. These techniques can activate memories and enhance clarity of thought, allowing for a more profound understanding of the content documented in your journals. As you breathe deeply and focus on specific entries, you may find that certain memories surface more vividly, providing a clearer picture of your past and its impact on your present life. Integrating these methods into your analysis encourages a holistic approach, where physical, emotional, and cognitive aspects of memory retrieval work in harmony.

Finally, consider engaging in group workshops dedicated to shared memory exploration. Discussing journal entries in a supportive environment can yield collective insights and foster a sense of community. Participants may resonate with each other's experiences, triggering memories and reflections that contribute to individual and collective understanding. The communal aspect of sharing memories not only validates personal experiences but also enriches the overall journey of exploring repressed memories. By analyzing journal entries collaboratively, participants can unlock layers of their souls, revealing connections to past lives and deepening their spiritual journeys.

5

Meditation Techniques for Repressed Memories

Understanding Meditation and Memory

Meditation serves as a vital tool in the exploration of memory, especially when addressing repressed experiences and past life memories. By quieting the mind and fostering a deep state of awareness, individuals can access layers of consciousness that often remain obscured in the busyness of daily life. This practice creates a conducive environment for uncovering memories that may have been suppressed due to trauma or other emotional barriers. As believers in reincarnation and spiritual exploration, understanding how meditation enriches memory recall can significantly enhance personal journeys into the past.

The connection between meditation and memory lies in the ability to alter one's state of consciousness. During meditation, practitioners often experience transcendent states that allow for introspection and reflection. This altered state can facilitate the retrieval of memories that are otherwise difficult to access. Techniques such as mindfulness meditation, focused attention, and guided visualization can help practitioners delve into their subconscious, where past life memories may reside. Engaging with these techniques allows individuals to navigate through emotional blocks and fosters a deeper understanding of their spiritual journeys.

Incorporating meditation into memory retrieval practices can be particularly effective when used alongside journaling. After a meditation session, individuals can articulate their experiences and insights in written form, solidifying the memories accessed during the practice. Journaling serves not only as a record but also as a catalyst for further exploration. By documenting thoughts, feelings, and images that arise during meditation, practitioners can identify patterns or themes that may point to past life experiences or repressed emotions. This combination of meditation and journaling enriches the process of self-discovery and memory recall.

Moreover, specific meditation techniques, including breathwork and visualization, can enhance memory activation. Breathwork, in particular, is instrumental in calming the nervous system and allowing for deeper introspection. As the breath becomes a focal point, it facilitates a sense of grounding that can unlock memories stored within the body. Guided visualizations can also create vivid imagery that resonates with personal experiences, helping individuals to connect with their past lives or repressed memories. By employing these techniques, practitioners can create a holistic approach to memory recall that integrates mind, body, and spirit.

Finally, group workshops that incorporate meditation can amplify the experience of memory exploration. Sharing insights and experiences within a supportive community fosters an environment of trust and openness, enabling deeper connections to emerge. Collective meditative practices can lead to shared memories or insights that may not surface during individual sessions. By engaging with others who share similar beliefs and experiences, individuals can enhance their understanding of memory and its intricate relationship with the soul's journey across lifetimes. Embracing meditation as a pathway to memory recall opens the door to profound spiritual insights and personal transformation.

Different Meditation Techniques for Memory Recall

Meditation serves as a powerful tool for enhancing memory recall, particularly for those seeking to explore repressed experiences and past life memories. Various techniques can facilitate this process, allowing individuals to tap into deeper levels of consciousness. Mindfulness meditation, for instance, encourages practitioners to focus on the present moment, fostering an awareness of thoughts and sensations without judgment. This heightened state of awareness can create a fertile ground for memory retrieval, as individuals learn to recognize and confront repressed memories that may surface during meditation.

Guided visualization is another effective approach, particularly for those interested in accessing past life memories. In this technique, a practitioner often listens to a facilitator who leads them through a vivid mental journey. By creating a safe and structured environment, guided visualization can help individuals relax and visualize scenes from their past lives. This allows for the emergence of specific memories tied to previous existences, providing insights that may have been buried deep within the subconscious. The imaginative process engages the mind in a way that can unlock memories that are otherwise inaccessible.

Breathwork is a complementary meditation technique that enhances memory recall by integrating physical and emotional experiences. Through controlled breathing exercises, individuals can enter altered states of consciousness that promote relaxation and emotional release. This practice not only aids in reducing anxiety and stress, which can hinder memory recall, but also encourages the body to process and release repressed memories. As participants engage in breathwork, they may find themselves recalling significant experiences that have shaped their past lives or present realities.

Art therapy, while distinct from traditional meditation, can also be viewed as a meditative practice that fosters memory exploration. By engaging in creative expression, individuals may inadvertently access memories and emotions tied to their past experiences. The act of creating art can serve as a meditative process, allowing for a deeper connection to one's inner self. This connection can unveil hidden memories and foster a greater understanding of repressed emotions, facilitating the exploration of past lives and experiences that may have been long forgotten.

Finally, group workshops focused on shared memory exploration can enhance the process of memory recall through collective energy and support. In a communal setting, participants often feel a sense of safety that encourages vulnerability. This environment can stimulate discussions and reflections that may trigger personal recollections of repressed memories. The shared experiences and insights gained from others can provide new perspectives, making it easier for individuals to access their own past life memories. As participants engage in collective meditation practices, the synergy of the group can amplify individual recall abilities, creating a transformative experience for all involved.

Creating a Meditation Practice for Memory Exploration

Creating a meditation practice for memory exploration involves cultivating a dedicated space and time for reflection, enabling individuals to access deeper layers of consciousness. This practice begins with setting intentions that align with personal goals for memory recall, particularly concerning repressed experiences or past life memories. By establishing clear objectives, practitioners can focus their meditative efforts on specific themes or questions that resonate with their spiritual journeys. The sacred space for meditation should be serene and free from distractions, allowing for a profound connection with the inner self.

Guided visualization can serve as a powerful tool in this meditation practice, helping individuals navigate through layers of memory. By employing imagery and narrative techniques, practitioners can create vivid landscapes of their past experiences, facilitating a journey into the subconscious. This process often leads to significant insights, as participants visualize scenarios that may unlock repressed memories. Incorporating sound, such as calming music or nature sounds, can enhance the experience, enabling deeper relaxation and receptivity to the memories being explored.

Journaling complements meditation by providing a tangible means to document insights and experiences that arise during sessions. After each meditation, individuals should take time to write down any revelations or feelings encountered. This practice not only reinforces memory recall but also helps to identify patterns and themes over time. Journaling serves as a bridge between the meditative experience and everyday life, allowing for ongoing reflection and integration of insights gained from the subconscious.

Incorporating breathwork into the meditation practice can further enhance memory activation. By engaging in specific breathing techniques, individuals can cultivate a state of relaxation that promotes deeper access to repressed memories. Breathwork facilitates the release of tension and opens pathways for energy flow, which can lead to the emergence of suppressed experiences. This combination of meditation and breathwork creates a holistic approach to memory exploration, reinforcing the connection between mind, body, and spirit.

Lastly, group workshops can provide an invaluable support system for individuals engaged in memory exploration. Sharing experiences with like-minded individuals fosters a sense of community and validation. These workshops can include guided meditations, collaborative breathwork sessions, and discussions about insights gained, allowing participants to learn from one another. The collective energy and shared intentions amplify the potential for memory recall, offering a profound experience that transcends individual exploration and taps into the collective consciousness.

6

Hypnotherapy for Accessing Past Lives

The Basics of Hypnotherapy

Hypnotherapy serves as a powerful tool for those seeking to access and explore their deeper selves, particularly for individuals interested in reincarnation and spiritual experiences. At its core, hypnotherapy is a therapeutic technique that utilizes guided relaxation, intense concentration, and focused attention to achieve a heightened state of awareness known as trance. Within this state, individuals may become more open to exploring memories, sensations, and insights that lie beyond their ordinary conscious awareness. This makes hypnotherapy particularly beneficial for those wishing to retrieve repressed memories or delve into past life experiences.

The process often begins with a skilled hypnotherapist guiding the individual into a state of deep relaxation. Through techniques such as progressive muscle relaxation and visualization, the subject is encouraged to let go of external distractions and internal resistance. As the mind becomes more receptive, the hypnotherapist may use suggestions to facilitate access to memories that may not be readily available in a waking state. This can include imagery and sensory experiences related to past lives or significant emotional memories that have been repressed due to trauma or other factors.

One of the key mechanisms of hypnotherapy is its ability to bypass the critical faculties of the conscious mind, allowing for deeper exploration of the subconscious. For believers in reincarnation and spiritualist practices, this aspect is crucial, as it can lead to profound revelations about past life experiences. Individuals may find themselves recalling vivid details of historical circumstances, relationships, and emotions that resonate with their current life. This connection can foster a sense of continuity and understanding regarding their current challenges and behaviors.

In addition to facilitating memory retrieval, hypnotherapy also serves as a therapeutic vehicle for healing. By uncovering and processing repressed memories, individuals can confront unresolved emotions and traumas that have impacted their present lives. This healing aspect is particularly significant for those who have experienced alien abduction or other extraordinary events, as it allows for a safe exploration of these experiences in a supportive environment. The insights gained through hypnotherapy can lead to a greater sense of self-awareness and empowerment, enabling individuals to integrate these experiences into their broader spiritual journey.

Ultimately, hypnotherapy is a versatile practice that aligns well with various memory recall techniques, including guided visualization and art therapy. It can be effectively combined with other methods such as neuro-linguistic programming and breathwork to enhance memory activation and retrieval. For those engaged in group workshops or spiritual practices aimed at uncovering hidden memories, hypnotherapy can serve as a foundational tool that deepens the exploration of shared experiences. By unlocking the subconscious, hypnotherapy helps individuals connect with their pasts, fostering healing, understanding, and transformation in their spiritual journeys.

Hypnotherapy Techniques for Past Life Recall

Hypnotherapy techniques for past life recall serve as a powerful tool for individuals seeking to explore the depths of their souls and uncover hidden memories that may span beyond their current existence. By accessing altered states of consciousness, hypnotherapy allows individuals to bypass the conscious mind's filters and tap into the subconscious, where repressed experiences and past life memories reside. Practitioners often utilize guided imagery and relaxation techniques to create a safe environment, facilitating a deep state of relaxation that encourages exploration of one's past lives.

One of the primary techniques used in hypnotherapy for past life recall is regression therapy. During a regression session, the therapist guides the individual back to previous lifetimes by using prompts and suggestions designed to evoke vivid memories. This process often involves focusing on specific life themes, relationships, or unresolved issues that may carry over from past lives. As the individual navigates through these memories, they may encounter significant events, relationships, and challenges that provide insight into their current life struggles, fears, or desires.

In addition to regression therapy, practitioners may incorporate elements of guided visualization, allowing clients to create mental images that represent their past life experiences. This technique enables individuals to experience memories more vividly, as they visualize the settings, people, and emotions associated with their past lives.

By engaging multiple senses during the visualization process, clients can enhance their recall and deepen their understanding of how these past experiences influence their present reality. Journaling practices can further complement this process, as writing about recalled memories often solidifies and clarifies insights gained during hypnotherapy sessions.

Meditation techniques are also frequently utilized in conjunction with hypnotherapy to access repressed memories. By encouraging a meditative state, individuals become more receptive to the subconscious, allowing memories to surface naturally. Breathwork practices can enhance this meditative state, facilitating deeper relaxation and opening pathways to memory activation. The combination of breath control and focused intent can help individuals reach a heightened state of awareness, conducive to uncovering past life experiences that might otherwise remain hidden.

Ultimately, the integration of hypnotherapy techniques with other memory recall practices creates a holistic approach to exploring past lives. Whether through art therapy, dream analysis, or group workshops, each modality can provide unique insights into the individual's journey. As believers in reincarnation and spiritualists seek to understand their soul's history, hypnotherapy offers a structured yet flexible framework for delving into the mysteries of their past, fostering healing and personal growth in the process.

Safety and Ethics in Hypnotherapy

In the realm of hypnotherapy, safety and ethics are paramount, particularly when working with individuals seeking to uncover repressed or past life memories. Practitioners must create a secure environment that fosters trust and ensures the well-being of clients throughout the process. This involves maintaining a professional demeanor, obtaining informed consent, and clearly communicating the goals of the sessions. Building rapport is essential, as clients are often vulnerable when exploring deeply personal and sometimes traumatic experiences. A responsible hypnotherapist prioritizes the emotional and psychological safety of clients, ensuring they feel supported and understood.

Ethical considerations extend beyond the therapeutic relationship to encompass the methods employed during hypnotherapy. It is vital for practitioners to utilize techniques that are evidence-based and aligned with the best practices in the field. This includes being aware of the potential for false memories to arise during sessions, which can complicate the therapeutic process. Hypnotherapists must be trained to discern genuine memories from those that may be inadvertently suggested. This requires a commitment to ongoing education and supervision, ensuring that practitioners remain updated on the latest developments in memory recall and hypnotherapy ethics.

In addition to the individual safety of clients, hypnotherapists must also consider the broader implications of their work on the community. This involves respecting the diverse beliefs and experiences of clients, particularly those within the spiritualist and reincarnation belief systems. Practitioners should approach each session with cultural sensitivity, recognizing that concepts of memory, identity, and the soul may differ significantly among individuals. By honoring these differences, hypnotherapists can enhance the therapeutic experience and foster a more profound understanding of the client's journey.

Furthermore, confidentiality plays a crucial role in maintaining ethical standards within hypnotherapy. Clients must feel assured that their experiences and memories, especially those related to past lives or repressed memories, will be treated with the utmost discretion. Practitioners should clearly outline confidentiality policies and the limits thereof, particularly in group settings where shared experiences may occur. This transparency helps to create a safe space for exploration and encourages clients to engage more fully with the therapeutic process.

Ultimately, the intersection of safety and ethics in hypnotherapy is vital for facilitating genuine memory recall and exploration of repressed experiences. As practitioners guide clients through their journeys of self-discovery, it is essential to uphold the highest standards of integrity, compassion, and professionalism. By doing so, hypnotherapists not only empower individuals to unlock their past but also contribute to a broader understanding of the intricate relationship between memory, identity, and spiritual growth.

7

Art Therapy for Exploring Repressed Experiences

The Therapeutic Benefits of Art

The therapeutic benefits of art extend beyond mere expression; they serve as a vital tool for individuals seeking to unlock repressed memories and connect with their past lives. Engaging in artistic activities provides a unique avenue for exploration, allowing practitioners to access emotions and experiences that may be deeply buried within the subconscious. Through painting, drawing, or sculpting, individuals can tap into memories associated with previous incarnations, facilitating a dialogue between the conscious and subconscious mind. This creative process not only encourages self-discovery but also fosters healing by bringing to the surface feelings that may otherwise remain unaddressed.

Art therapy serves as a powerful mechanism for those who believe in reincarnation, as it provides a non-verbal means of expression. Many individuals find that words alone cannot encapsulate the depth of their experiences. Art allows for the manifestation of these complex emotions, often revealing insights about past lives that may not be readily accessible through traditional memory recall techniques. The act of creating art can evoke feelings of nostalgia, recognition, and sometimes even trauma, all of which can lead to significant breakthroughs in understanding one's spiritual journey and past life connections.

Incorporating guided visualization techniques with art can enhance the therapeutic experience. As participants engage in visualizing specific past life scenarios, they can simultaneously express these visions through artistic means. This dual approach of visualization and creation can deepen the connection to past experiences, allowing for a richer understanding of one's soul's journey. By focusing on imagery that resonates with their spiritual beliefs, individuals can unlock memories that have shaped their current existence, reinforcing the interconnectedness of their past and present.

Additionally, group workshops centered around art therapy can create a supportive community environment where individuals share their artistic expressions and insights. This collective space fosters a sense of belonging and validation, essential for those exploring their spiritual and reincarnational beliefs. Participants can engage in discussions about their creations, facilitating a deeper understanding of shared experiences and the collective unconscious. The act of witnessing each other's art can also validate personal journeys, encouraging individuals to explore even deeper layers of their consciousness.

Finally, incorporating breathwork and meditation into art therapy sessions can further enhance the process of memory activation. Breathwork helps to center the mind and body, creating a conducive environment for exploration. When combined with the free expression of art, individuals may find it easier to access repressed memories and insights. This holistic approach not only promotes mental clarity but also aligns the individual's spiritual self with their creative expression, helping to unlock the soul's narrative woven through time, and ultimately contributing to the healing journey of those exploring their past lives.

Art Techniques for Memory Exploration

Art techniques serve as powerful tools for memory exploration, particularly for those seeking to unlock repressed experiences and past life memories. Engaging with creative mediums allows individuals to bypass the constraints of verbal expression, tapping into the subconscious where hidden memories often reside. This chapter delves into various art techniques that can enhance memory recall, providing a supportive framework for spiritual seekers and those who resonate with the concepts of reincarnation and past life exploration.

One effective method is expressive painting, which encourages individuals to convey their emotions and memories through color and form. The process of creating art can facilitate a deeper connection to the self, allowing for the emergence of visual representations of repressed experiences. Participants are often surprised by the imagery that surfaces, as it may reveal fragments of past lives or significant moments that have been obscured. The freedom of expression inherent in this technique can lead to profound insights and emotional release, making it a compelling avenue for memory exploration.

Drawing and sketching also play a vital role in artistic memory recall. By encouraging individuals to illustrate memories or feelings associated with their past, they can access deeper layers of consciousness. This technique fosters a dialogue between the mind and the body, as the act of drawing can activate neural pathways associated with memory. As individuals engage in this process, they may uncover symbols or themes that resonate with their spiritual beliefs, illuminating connections to their past experiences and spiritual journeys.

Collage-making is another dynamic technique that combines various materials to create a visual narrative. This approach allows individuals to curate images, textures, and words that reflect their inner experiences and memories. By piecing together different elements, participants can construct a holistic representation of their past, facilitating discoveries that may be difficult to articulate through traditional means. Collage can serve as a tangible artifact of the memory exploration process, providing a visual representation of the insights gained during artistic creation.

Finally, incorporating performance art or movement into memory exploration can further enhance the retrieval of repressed experiences. Engaging the body through dance or improvisational movement allows for the release of pent-up emotions and memories stored within the physical form. This kinesthetic approach can unlock memories that may be inaccessible through cognitive methods, offering a profound way to connect with one's past lives. By embracing these art techniques, individuals can embark on a transformative journey toward understanding their hidden memories, ultimately leading to greater self-awareness and spiritual growth.

Interpreting Art as a Reflection of Memory

Art serves as a profound medium through which individuals can explore and express the complex interplay between memory and identity. For those who believe in reincarnation and the exploration of past lives, art becomes a canvas that reflects not just the conscious experiences of the present, but also the echoes of memories long repressed. By interpreting art—be it through painting, sculpture, or performance—individuals can gain insight into their subconscious, unveiling layers of memory that may have been obscured by time and trauma. This process is particularly significant for spiritualists and those who seek to uncover the truths of their past lives, as it allows for a deeper connection to the essence of the soul's journey across different incarnations.

The act of creating art can serve as a powerful tool in memory recall techniques. Engaging in artistic expression encourages a meditative state that can facilitate access to repressed experiences. As individuals immerse themselves in the creative process, they often find that emotions and memories surface organically. This can be particularly beneficial in group workshops where shared experiences amplify personal revelations. The collective energy and support of a group can foster a safe environment for exploration, enabling participants to tap into communal memories that may resonate with their own past lives. Thus, art becomes not merely a reflection of the artist's current state but an exploration of the collective consciousness that spans generations and lifetimes.

Art therapy, in particular, has emerged as a valuable practice for exploring repressed experiences. It allows individuals to externalize their internal struggles and confront memories that may be painful or difficult to access through traditional verbal methods. By interpreting their artistic creations, individuals can gain clarity on their emotional responses, recognizing patterns that may correlate with past life experiences. This therapeutic approach aligns well with the practices of guided visualization and meditation, where imagery and symbolism play crucial roles in accessing deeper layers of the psyche. Both art and these techniques serve to bridge the gap between the conscious and subconscious, facilitating a journey towards healing and understanding.

Breathwork and dream analysis further enhance the relationship between art and memory. Breathwork can induce altered states of consciousness, allowing individuals to enter a state where memories can be more readily accessed. During these sessions, participants may feel inspired to create art that captures fleeting sensations or visions experienced during their practice. Similarly, dream analysis can unveil insights that might inform their artistic endeavors. Dreams often encapsulate themes and symbols from past lives, and by interpreting these dreams, individuals can create artwork that reflects their subconscious explorations, thus further integrating their experiences into their conscious lives.

Ultimately, the interpretation of art as a reflection of memory not only enriches the individual's understanding of themselves but also fosters a sense of connection to a larger narrative. For believers in reincarnation and spiritual exploration, each piece of art becomes a chapter in the ongoing story of the soul. By engaging with various techniques—such as hypnotherapy, journaling, and neuro-linguistic programming—individuals can enhance their ability to recall and articulate these past experiences. As they do so, they contribute to a broader dialogue about memory, identity, and the intricate tapestry of life that transcends time and space. Through art, memories become not just personal artifacts but shared experiences that illuminate the universal journey of the soul.

8

Breathwork for Memory Activation

The Science of Breath and Memory

The connection between breath and memory is an intricate one, grounded in both ancient wisdom and modern science. Breath is not merely a physiological function; it serves as a bridge between the conscious and subconscious mind. When we engage in controlled breathing techniques, we can enter altered states of consciousness that facilitate memory recall. For those on a spiritual path, including believers in reincarnation and those exploring past life memories, understanding this connection can unlock profound insights into forgotten experiences.

Research in neuroscience has shown that breath regulation can influence brain activity, especially in the areas responsible for memory processing. For instance, practices such as breathwork can increase oxygen flow to the brain, enhancing cognitive functions and promoting emotional regulation. This increase in oxygen can activate neural pathways that may have been dormant, allowing individuals to access repressed memories or even past life experiences. By focusing on the rhythm and depth of breathing, one can create a conducive environment for memory retrieval, making it an essential tool for those seeking to explore their spiritual histories.

Guided visualization, often paired with breathwork, serves as a powerful technique for accessing past life memories. By combining deep, rhythmic breathing with visual imagery, individuals can navigate the layers of their subconscious, revealing hidden narratives that shape their current lives. In a safe and supportive setting, participants can journey through time, encountering significant events, relationships, and lessons from previous incarnations. This practice not only fosters personal growth but also encourages a deeper connection to one's spiritual essence.

Moreover, journaling practices complement breathwork and visualization by providing a structured way to process and articulate recalled memories. Writing can serve as a cathartic release, allowing for the exploration of emotions and insights that arise during memory recall sessions. When combined with breath-focused meditation, journaling becomes a dynamic tool for reflecting on experiences, identifying patterns, and integrating lessons learned from past lives. This practice can enhance one's understanding of their spiritual journey, creating a cohesive narrative that links past and present.

In group workshops, shared breathwork and memory exploration can foster community and collective healing. Engaging in breath-based activities in a supportive environment can amplify the effects of memory recall, as participants share their experiences and insights. This communal aspect not only validates individual journeys but also encourages a sense of interconnectedness among those exploring similar paths. As the science of breath continues to reveal its potential, the integration of these practices provides a holistic approach to uncovering the depths of memory, paving the way for profound spiritual awakening and personal transformation.

Breathwork Techniques for Activation

Breathwork techniques serve as powerful tools for activation and memory recall, particularly for those exploring the depths of their past lives and repressed experiences. At the core of these techniques lies the understanding that breath is not merely a physiological function but a bridge to altered states of consciousness. By engaging in conscious breathwork, individuals can tap into deeper layers of their psyche, facilitating access to memories that may have been buried or forgotten. This process empowers practitioners to confront and integrate significant past experiences, thereby unlocking insights that resonate with their spiritual journey.

One effective approach to breathwork is the practice of circular breathing, which involves a continuous flow of inhalation and exhalation without pauses. This technique can induce a state of altered consciousness, allowing practitioners to bypass the analytical mind and access deeper emotional states. During sessions, individuals may experience vivid memories or sensations linked to past life experiences. The rhythmic nature of circular breathing helps to quiet the mind, creating a safe space for exploration. This technique can be enhanced by pairing it with guided visualizations that focus on specific memories or themes related to past lives, further facilitating the recall process.

Another impactful method is the use of breath retention, or Kumbhaka, which encourages individuals to hold their breath for short periods. This practice can heighten awareness and sensitivity to internal experiences, often leading to revelations about repressed memories. By creating a moment of stillness within the breath, practitioners may find that they are more attuned to subtle feelings and sensations that arise, which may be connected to significant past life events. Integrating this technique with journaling practices allows individuals to document their experiences immediately after sessions, ensuring that insights are captured and explored further.

Integrating breathwork within group workshops can amplify its effectiveness. The supportive energy of a group creates a collective field that enhances individual experiences. Participants can share their insights, fostering a sense of community and collective healing. Group breathwork sessions often lead to synchronized breathing patterns, which can deepen the group's connection to shared memories or themes. This communal approach not only aids in memory recall but also reinforces the idea that individuals are part of a larger tapestry of existence, woven through time and across lifetimes.

Lastly, combining breathwork with other therapeutic modalities such as hypnotherapy and art therapy can yield profound insights. Breathwork can serve as a preparatory practice, calming the mind and body before delving into deeper therapeutic work. Art therapy, when used alongside breathwork, allows individuals to express their recalled memories through creative means, facilitating a holistic exploration of their experiences. By engaging multiple senses and modalities, practitioners can enhance their journey toward memory activation, ultimately leading to a richer understanding of their soul's path across lifetimes.

Integrating Breathwork into Daily Practice

Integrating breathwork into daily practice serves as a powerful tool for those seeking to unlock the depths of their soul and access repressed experiences, particularly regarding past life memories. Breathwork, a practice rooted in various spiritual traditions, involves intentional breathing techniques that can enhance awareness and facilitate deeper states of consciousness. For believers in reincarnation and spiritualists, incorporating breathwork into daily routines can create a sacred space for reflection and exploration, allowing individuals to connect more profoundly with their inner selves and the memories that lie beneath the surface.

To begin the integration of breathwork, individuals should establish a consistent practice that aligns with their personal routines. Setting aside dedicated time each day, whether in the morning to prepare for the day ahead or in the evening to reflect on the experiences of the day, can create a structured approach. Simple techniques such as diaphragmatic breathing or box breathing can be easily incorporated, providing a foundation for deeper exploration. As practitioners become comfortable with these techniques, they can gradually introduce more advanced breathwork methods that facilitate emotional release and memory activation, enhancing their ability to recall past life experiences.

Guided breathwork sessions can further enhance the efficacy of this practice. Engaging in group workshops or online sessions led by experienced practitioners allows individuals to experience collective energy, which can amplify the effects of breathwork. These sessions often incorporate visualization techniques that encourage participants to journey into their subconscious, probing for hidden memories and insights. The combination of breath control and guided imagery creates a fertile environment for uncovering layers of the self that may have remained dormant, making breathwork a vital component of memory recall practices.

In addition to group settings, journaling can complement breathwork practices, allowing individuals to document their experiences and insights. After engaging in breathwork, allocating time to write about sensations, emotions, and any memories that arise can deepen the integration of the experience. This reflective process not only solidifies the memories accessed during breathwork but also provides a tangible record of personal progress in memory retrieval. By revisiting these journal entries, practitioners can track their journey and observe patterns that may emerge over time, further facilitating the exploration of repressed experiences.

As practitioners continue to weave breathwork into their daily lives, the cumulative effects can lead to profound transformations. Regular practice fosters a heightened state of awareness, enabling individuals to navigate their emotional landscapes with greater ease. By accessing repressed memories and insights through breathwork, believers in reincarnation and spiritualists can unlock the mysteries of their past lives, enriching their spiritual journey. Ultimately, integrating breathwork into daily practice not only serves as a path to memory retrieval but also as a means of cultivating a deeper connection with the soul.

9

Dream Analysis for Past Life Insights

The Role of Dreams in Memory Recall

Dreams serve as a vital conduit through which the subconscious mind expresses repressed experiences and insights, particularly for those exploring past lives and spiritual dimensions. In the realm of memory recall, dreams can act as a repository of forgotten memories, allowing individuals to access fragments of experiences that may not be available during waking hours. This phenomenon is especially relevant for believers in reincarnation and spiritual exploration, as dreams can bridge the gap between the conscious self and the deeper soul history that resides within. Engaging with dreams can reveal not only personal narratives but also universal themes connected to past life experiences, encouraging a deeper understanding of one's spiritual journey.

The process of dream recall is intricately linked to various memory techniques, including guided visualization and journaling practices. By setting intentions before sleep, individuals can direct their subconscious to retrieve specific memories during the dream state. Upon waking, journaling these dreams becomes essential; it not only aids in solidifying the recall but also allows for reflection and analysis of the symbols and narratives encountered. This practice fosters a dialogue between the conscious and subconscious, where insights gained during dreams can illuminate hidden aspects of one's past lives and repressed memories, facilitating a more profound healing process.

Meditation techniques play a crucial role in enhancing dream recall. Regular meditation cultivates a heightened state of awareness and prepares the mind for deeper exploration into the subconscious. By creating a calm mental space, practitioners can more easily navigate the dream landscape and access the messages waiting to be uncovered. Furthermore, integrating breathwork into meditation can amplify this effect, as controlled breathing helps to relax the body and mind, making it easier to enter a dream state conducive to memory retrieval. This combination of practices not only enhances the quality of dreams but also encourages the emergence of memories that may have been obscured by time or trauma.

Hypnotherapy represents another powerful tool for accessing past lives and repressed memories, often utilizing dreams as a springboard for exploration. Through guided sessions, individuals can enter altered states of consciousness where they can safely revisit past experiences, often leading to significant revelations. The insights gained during these sessions can be further examined through dream analysis, providing additional layers of understanding regarding the memories surfaced. This synergistic approach enhances the recall process and enriches the individual's spiritual journey by connecting the dots between past and present experiences.

Engaging in group workshops focused on shared memory exploration can also amplify the dream recall process. Such environments foster community and support, encouraging participants to share their dreams and the insights they glean from them. This collective exploration not only validates individual experiences but also allows for the pooling of interpretations and perspectives, enriching the overall understanding of past life memories. As participants engage with techniques such as neuro-linguistic programming and art therapy, they can enhance their ability to access and interpret memories, ultimately unlocking deeper layers of their soul's journey and the lessons embedded within their dreams.

Techniques for Dream Analysis

Dream analysis serves as a vital tool for individuals seeking to uncover the hidden layers of their psyche, specifically those exploring past life memories and repressed experiences. By delving into the symbolic language of dreams, practitioners can gain insights that transcend the ordinary. This technique involves interpreting the imagery, emotions, and narratives that arise during dream states, allowing for a deeper understanding of one's spiritual journey and potential past life experiences. The subconscious often communicates through dreams, offering clues that can guide individuals toward recalling significant memories.

One effective method for analyzing dreams is to maintain a dream journal. This practice encourages individuals to document their dreams immediately upon waking, capturing the nuances and feelings associated with each experience. Over time, patterns and recurring themes may emerge, providing a framework for interpreting their significance. For those interested in past life memories, noting specific symbols or characters that appear in dreams can lead to revelations about previous incarnations. This journaling practice not only enhances memory recall but also fosters a connection with the subconscious, facilitating a richer understanding of personal history.

Guided visualization techniques can further enhance dream analysis. By employing visualization exercises prior to sleep, individuals can set intentions for their dreams, inviting specific memories or insights related to past lives. These sessions can be structured to include affirmations or questions that the dreamer wishes to explore. The resulting dreams may yield profound insights, as the mind is more attuned to exploring themes relevant to the dreamer's spiritual journey. This technique bridges the conscious and subconscious, allowing for a seamless exploration of repressed memories and past life experiences.

Meditation serves as another powerful tool for dream analysis. Engaging in meditation before sleep can calm the mind and create an optimal environment for dream recall. During meditation, individuals can focus on questions or themes they wish to explore in their dreams, encouraging the subconscious to present relevant images or narratives. The practice of mindfulness during meditation can also enhance the clarity of dream recollection, allowing dreamers to better discern their dreams' meanings and implications for their lives and spiritual paths.

Lastly, participating in group workshops focused on dream analysis can provide a supportive space for shared exploration. These workshops often facilitate discussions and activities that encourage participants to share their dreams and insights, creating a collective atmosphere of discovery. The group dynamic can enhance individual understanding, as others' interpretations and experiences can shed light on personal dreams. This collaborative approach not only enriches the dream analysis process but also fosters a sense of community among those on similar spiritual journeys, reinforcing the interconnectedness of all experiences and memories.

Case Studies of Dreams and Past Life Insights

The exploration of dreams as a gateway to unlocking past life insights has captivated the minds of many who believe in reincarnation and spiritual experiences. Case studies reveal how individuals have encountered vivid dreams that serve as windows into their previous existences. For instance, one individual reported recurring dreams of a battlefield, replete with historical details that they later confirmed through research. These dreams not only provided a narrative of a life lived long ago but also offered emotional clarity, allowing the dreamer to process unresolved feelings tied to trauma from that past existence. Such experiences illustrate the potential of dream analysis as a tool for accessing hidden memories and understanding one's soul journey.

Guided visualization techniques further enhance the ability to access past life memories through dreams. In one notable case, a participant in a guided session experienced a profound recollection of a life as a healer in an ancient civilization. The imagery evoked during the session unfolded a rich tapestry of sensory details that felt both foreign and familiar. The subsequent journaling practice allowed the individual to articulate these experiences, leading to a deeper understanding of their current life's purpose. This case emphasizes the importance of structured techniques in facilitating memory retrieval and highlights how dreams can intertwine with guided experiences to unlock valuable insights.

Group workshops have also proven to be effective settings for shared memory exploration, where participants exchange dream experiences that may resonate with one another. In a recent workshop, participants were encouraged to describe their dreams related to past lives, which led to unexpected connections. One participant's dream of sailing across an ocean aligned with another's recollection of a life spent as a navigator in a bygone era. This collective sharing not only validated individual experiences but also fostered a sense of communal support, reinforcing the belief that these memories are interconnected. Such dynamics can catalyze group healing and collective memory activation, providing a richer understanding of the shared human experience.

Hypnotherapy has emerged as a powerful method for accessing past life memories, often revealing startling insights through the lens of dreams. A case study involving a hypnotherapy session revealed that a client's phobia of water stemmed from a traumatic drowning in a previous life. During the session, the client was able to visualize the dream-like scenario leading to the memory recall, enabling them to confront the underlying fear and release it through therapeutic techniques. This illustrates not only the effectiveness of hypnotherapy in unlocking repressed memories but also the profound impact of addressing past traumas on current emotional well-being.

Finally, the integration of art therapy has offered yet another dimension in exploring repressed experiences tied to past lives. In one case, an individual used painting to express the emotions stirred by a series of dreams depicting a life as an artist in the Renaissance. The act of creation became a therapeutic outlet, allowing the individual to process complex feelings of loss and longing associated with that life. This unique approach demonstrates the multifaceted ways in which memory recall techniques can be applied, emphasizing that the journey to uncovering hidden memories is not only about recollection but also about healing and self-discovery.

10

Group Workshops for Shared Memory Exploration

The Benefits of Group Exploration

Group exploration offers a unique and enriching experience for individuals seeking to unlock repressed memories or delve into past life recollections. Engaging with others in a supportive environment fosters a sense of community and shared purpose, which can significantly enhance the process of memory recall. Participants benefit from the collective energy and diverse perspectives that arise during group sessions, creating a fertile ground for personal insights and revelations. This collaborative approach not only encourages the sharing of experiences but also validates individual journeys, making participants feel less isolated in their explorations.

As individuals engage in guided visualization or meditation techniques within a group setting, the synergy created can amplify the effectiveness of these practices. The shared focus on a specific intention, such as accessing past life memories, can help participants break through mental blocks and reach deeper states of consciousness. Moreover, the presence of fellow explorers can provide comfort and reassurance, allowing individuals to navigate their experiences with greater ease. The communal aspect of group exploration can also encourage participants to be more open and vulnerable, leading to richer and more profound insights.

Journaling practices conducted in a group context can further enhance memory retrieval. Participants can share prompts and reflections, sparking new ideas and connections that may not arise in solitary writing. The act of articulating experiences and thoughts in the presence of others can help individuals process their memories more effectively, as feedback and encouragement from peers can inspire deeper exploration. This collaborative journaling can also reveal common themes and patterns, enriching the collective understanding of past experiences and their significance.

Art therapy within a group setting offers another powerful avenue for exploring repressed memories and past life experiences. Participants can express their emotions and insights through creative mediums, often uncovering memories that may be difficult to articulate verbally. The group dynamic allows for a safe space where individuals can share their artistic expressions, fostering a sense of belonging and acceptance. This mutual support can lead to transformative breakthroughs, as participants witness the diverse ways in which others interpret their experiences and emotions.

Ultimately, group workshops designed for shared memory exploration can significantly enhance the journey of uncovering hidden memories. By combining techniques such as hypnotherapy, breathwork, and dream analysis, participants can navigate the complexities of their pasts in a structured yet flexible environment. The collective wisdom and shared experiences of the group can facilitate deeper understanding and acceptance of each individual's unique path. As participants embark on this journey together, they not only unlock their own souls but also contribute to a greater collective consciousness, fostering healing and growth for all involved.

Structuring a Memory Recall Workshop

Structuring a memory recall workshop requires a thoughtful approach that integrates various techniques to cater to the diverse needs of participants, particularly those interested in past life experiences and spiritual exploration. The workshop should begin with a clear objective, providing an overview of the methodologies that will be employed. This introduction sets the tone and prepares participants for the journey ahead, creating a safe and welcoming environment conducive to deep introspection and memory retrieval.

The first segment of the workshop can focus on guided visualization, an effective method for accessing repressed memories. Participants will be led through a series of meditative exercises designed to relax the mind and open the channels to their subconscious. This phase should incorporate gentle music and calming imagery to facilitate a deeper connection with their inner selves. Encouraging participants to embrace their feelings and thoughts during these visualizations is essential, as it fosters a sense of trust in the process and in the group dynamics.

Following the guided visualization, participants can engage in journaling practices aimed at solidifying their experiences. Providing prompts that encourage reflection on the visualization can help participants articulate their insights. Journaling serves as both a tool for memory retrieval and a means of processing emotions that may arise during the workshop. It's important to create an atmosphere where participants feel comfortable sharing their writings, as this can enhance collective learning and validation of experiences.

Next, incorporating art therapy can provide an additional layer of exploration. Participants can be invited to express their experiences through drawing, painting, or other creative mediums. This artistic expression allows for the release of emotions and can reveal aspects of memory that may be difficult to articulate verbally. Facilitators should encourage participants to share their creations, fostering a sense of community and support among individuals who may have faced similar challenges in accessing their memories.

Finally, the workshop can conclude with a group discussion, allowing participants to share their experiences and insights. This collaborative aspect not only helps reinforce the memories accessed during the workshop but also promotes a sense of belonging among those who might feel isolated in their experiences. Providing resources for continued exploration, such as recommended readings or follow-up sessions, can empower participants to further their journey in uncovering hidden memories and understanding their past lives.

Facilitating Safe Spaces for Sharing

Creating safe spaces for sharing is crucial in the exploration of repressed memories and past life experiences. These environments not only foster trust but also encourage individuals to express their experiences without fear of judgment. For those engaged in spiritual practices, such as believers in reincarnation or participants in group workshops, the significance of a supportive atmosphere cannot be overstated. A safe space allows for the vulnerable act of sharing personal narratives, which can lead to profound insights and healing.

To facilitate these safe spaces, it is essential to establish ground rules that promote respect and confidentiality. Participants should feel assured that their stories will be held in confidence, allowing them to open up about their experiences, whether they involve memories of past lives or encounters perceived as extraterrestrial. Facilitators can encourage active listening, where each participant is given the opportunity to share without interruption. This practice not only validates individual experiences but also cultivates a sense of community among those exploring similar themes.

Incorporating various memory recall techniques can enhance the sharing process within these spaces. Guided visualizations can help participants tap into their past experiences more effectively, providing a structured approach to memory retrieval. Journaling practices can also be utilized before group sessions, encouraging individuals to articulate their thoughts and feelings in writing. This preparatory step can make sharing in a group setting less daunting and more meaningful, as individuals can reference their written insights during discussions.

Meditation and breathwork can serve as powerful tools to create a calm and receptive environment. These practices help participants center themselves, making it easier to access deeper memories and experiences. By integrating these techniques into the group dynamic, participants can experience a collective energy that enhances their ability to connect with their inner selves and with one another. This shared experience can lead to unexpected revelations and a deeper understanding of each individual's journey.

Finally, it is important to acknowledge and honor the diverse backgrounds and beliefs of all participants. Understanding that each person's experiences are valid, regardless of their origins, fosters an inclusive atmosphere. Facilitators should encourage openness to various interpretations of experiences, whether they stem from spiritual beliefs, psychological perspectives, or creative expressions through art therapy. By embracing this diversity, safe spaces for sharing can truly become sanctuaries for exploration and healing, enabling individuals to unlock the depths of their souls and discover the memories that shape their existence.

11

Neuro-Linguistic Programming for Memory

Understanding NLP and Its Application

NLP, or Neuro-Linguistic Programming, serves as a bridge between our cognitive processes and emotional experiences, offering profound insights into how we can access and enhance our memories, including those that may be repressed or tied to past lives. At its core, NLP is centered on the understanding that language and behavior influence our mental states and experiences. By examining the intricate relationship between our thoughts, feelings, and language patterns, practitioners can develop techniques that facilitate memory recall and emotional healing, making it a valuable tool for individuals interested in spiritual growth and understanding their past lives.

In the context of memory recall, NLP employs specific strategies that can help individuals tap into their subconscious mind. Techniques such as anchoring and reframing allow practitioners to create associations that enhance their ability to recall past experiences, including memories that may be buried deep within. For believers in reincarnation and spiritualism, these methods can aid in unearthing significant past life experiences, providing clarity and insight into one's current life challenges. By utilizing NLP techniques, individuals can explore their past with greater depth, unlocking memories that contribute to their spiritual journey.

Guided visualization is another NLP technique that holds promise for those seeking to recover repressed memories. By inducing a relaxed state, practitioners can lead individuals through visual journeys that allow them to access their subconscious, revealing insights and memories that are otherwise inaccessible. This process can be particularly beneficial for alien abductees or individuals who feel disconnected from their past, as it creates a safe space to explore and understand the impact of these experiences. Through guided visualization, users can confront and integrate these memories, facilitating healing and personal growth.

Journaling practices, often enhanced by NLP, encourage individuals to articulate their thoughts and feelings related to their memories. This reflective process not only helps in organizing and processing experiences but also serves as a catalyst for deeper exploration. By employing specific language patterns and prompts rooted in NLP, individuals can unlock further layers of their consciousness, leading to a more profound understanding of their past lives. This practice aligns perfectly with the spiritualist approach to memory retrieval, where writing becomes a sacred act of discovery and connection to one's soul history.

Ultimately, the integration of NLP into memory recall techniques provides a multifaceted approach to exploring repressed and past life memories. By combining the principles of NLP with practices like meditation, hypnotherapy, and art therapy, individuals can create a comprehensive framework for accessing and understanding their hidden experiences. This holistic methodology not only enhances memory recall but also fosters a deeper connection to the self and the spiritual realm, guiding individuals on their path toward healing and enlightenment.

NLP Techniques for Memory Recall

NLP techniques for memory recall can be instrumental in unlocking repressed experiences, particularly for those who believe in reincarnation and past lives. Neuro-Linguistic Programming operates on the premise that language and neurological processes influence our thoughts and behaviors. By utilizing specific NLP strategies, individuals can enhance their ability to access and retrieve memories that may have been obscured by time or trauma. Techniques such as anchoring, reframing, and timeline therapy can create pathways to revisit past experiences, offering a deeper understanding of one's spiritual journey across lifetimes.

Anchoring is a fundamental NLP technique that involves associating a physical gesture or a specific word with an emotional state or memory. Practitioners can use this method to trigger recollections of past life experiences. By establishing a clear anchor, individuals can return to a state of openness and receptivity, making it easier to access memories that may have been buried. This technique not only aids in recall but also empowers individuals to manage their emotional responses to those memories, fostering a sense of control over their past.

Reframing, another powerful NLP technique, involves changing the way an individual perceives a memory or experience. For those exploring past lives, reframing can help transform negative associations with certain memories into more positive understandings. By viewing past events through a new lens, individuals can release emotional blockages and gain insights that facilitate healing. This process encourages a more compassionate perspective on one's experiences, allowing for a smoother integration of memories into the present consciousness.

Timeline therapy, a specialized NLP technique, allows individuals to visualize their life experiences along a temporal line. This method can be particularly useful in identifying and accessing past life memories by enabling practitioners to explore various points along their timeline. By reflecting on significant events or emotions, individuals can uncover hidden memories tied to previous incarnations. This technique promotes a greater sense of continuity and connection between past and present, reinforcing the belief in the cyclical nature of existence.

Incorporating NLP techniques into memory recall practices can significantly enhance the journey of self-discovery for those interested in exploring past lives. By combining these approaches with other methods such as guided visualization, meditation, and journaling, individuals can create a comprehensive toolkit for uncovering hidden memories. This multifaceted approach encourages a deeper exploration of the self, ultimately enriching one's understanding of their spiritual path and the lessons from their past experiences.

Enhancing Memory through Language Patterns

Enhancing memory through language patterns involves a deep understanding of how words and phrases can influence our cognitive processes, particularly in the context of recalling repressed experiences and past life memories. Language serves not only as a means of communication but also as a powerful tool for shaping our perceptions and enhancing our memory recall capabilities. By utilizing specific language patterns, individuals can create a conducive environment for accessing memories that may have remained dormant or obscured by time and trauma.

The use of guided visualization can significantly benefit those seeking to unlock their past life memories. Through carefully crafted narratives and descriptive language, participants can be led into a relaxed state where their subconscious mind becomes more accessible. This technique often involves the integration of sensory language, which enhances the vividness of the recalled experiences. As individuals engage with these visualizations, they may find that the emotions and sensations tied to their past lives come to the forefront, facilitating a deeper understanding of their current existence.

Journaling practices can further enhance memory retrieval by providing a structured outlet for expression and reflection. The act of writing itself can serve as a language pattern that organizes thoughts and feelings, making it easier to identify recurring themes or symbols associated with past experiences. By reflecting on these themes, individuals may uncover connections to their past lives that were previously unrecognized. Additionally, the written word allows for a tangible record of insights, which can be revisited and expanded upon over time, solidifying the memories in the conscious mind.

Meditation techniques, when combined with specific language cues, can also be instrumental in accessing repressed memories. Guided meditations that utilize affirmations and evocative language can help participants enter a deeper state of awareness, promoting the retrieval of hidden memories. The intentional use of language in meditation can create a resonance that aligns with spiritual practices, allowing for a harmonization of the mind and spirit. This alignment is crucial for those on a journey of self-discovery, as it facilitates a clearer pathway to understanding one's past lives.

Finally, the integration of neuro-linguistic programming (NLP) techniques can provide a nuanced approach to memory enhancement. NLP focuses on the relationship between language, behavior, and patterns of thought, making it an effective tool for those seeking to unlock their memories. By employing specific linguistic patterns, practitioners can help individuals reframe their experiences and beliefs surrounding their past lives. This reframing can lead to a more profound exploration of memory, as individuals begin to see their repressed experiences in a new light, ultimately fostering a richer understanding of their soul's journey.

12

Spiritual Practices for Uncovering Hidden Memories

Connecting Spirituality and Memory

Connecting spirituality and memory involves understanding the intricate relationship between our consciousness and the various dimensions of existence. For believers in reincarnation and spiritualism, memory serves as a bridge to past lives, allowing individuals to access experiences that may have been repressed due to trauma or other psychological barriers. This connection can be further explored through various memory recall techniques, which not only facilitate the retrieval of repressed memories but also deepen one's spiritual practice. By engaging with these techniques, individuals can unlock profound insights into their past, fostering a sense of continuity and purpose in their current lives.

Guided visualization is a powerful tool in this context, enabling practitioners to journey inward and access memories that may otherwise remain hidden. As individuals visualize specific scenarios or past life experiences, they can bypass the conscious mind's defenses and tap into the subconscious. This method encourages a relaxed state, making it easier to confront and process difficult emotions or memories. When combined with spiritual intentions, guided visualization can lead to significant breakthroughs, allowing individuals to reconcile past experiences with their current spiritual journey.

Journaling practices also play a crucial role in connecting spirituality with memory. Writing serves as a means of externalizing thoughts and emotions, providing clarity and structure to the often chaotic landscape of memory retrieval. By documenting memories that surface during spiritual practices, individuals can create a personal archive of insights and revelations. This practice not only aids in the recall of past life experiences but also encourages reflection on how these memories influence present behavior and beliefs. It can become a sacred ritual that deepens one's spiritual connection and understanding of the self.

Meditation techniques, particularly those focused on accessing repressed memories, can further enhance the connection between spirituality and memory. Through mindfulness and focused awareness, practitioners can enter altered states of consciousness where past experiences can emerge. These meditative states facilitate a deeper exploration of one's inner world, allowing individuals to confront suppressed emotions and memories in a safe and supportive environment.

As memories surface, they can be integrated into one's spiritual framework, enriching the individual's journey towards self-discovery and healing.

Incorporating other modalities such as hypnotherapy, art therapy, and breathwork can further enhance memory activation and retrieval. Each of these practices provides unique pathways to explore the depths of the subconscious mind, unlocking repressed memories and fostering spiritual growth. Group workshops also offer a communal space for shared memory exploration, allowing participants to connect with others on similar journeys. Ultimately, the intersection of spirituality and memory creates a rich tapestry of experiences that not only illuminate the past but also guide individuals towards a more profound understanding of their spiritual essence and purpose in this lifetime.

Spiritual Techniques for Memory Discovery

Spiritual techniques for memory discovery encompass a range of practices designed to facilitate the retrieval of repressed experiences and past life memories. For individuals who resonate with the concepts of reincarnation and spiritual exploration, these techniques offer pathways to access profound insights and understanding. Memory retrieval is not merely a cognitive exercise; it often involves engaging the spirit and the subconscious, enabling a holistic approach that honors the interconnectedness of mind, body, and spirit. This subchapter will explore various spiritual techniques that can aid in uncovering hidden memories and experiences.

Guided visualization stands out as a powerful tool for past life recall. This technique involves entering a deeply relaxed state, often facilitated by a guide or recorded session, which allows individuals to visualize scenarios and memories that might be locked away in their subconscious. During guided visualizations, practitioners may encounter vivid imagery or emotional sensations that lead to recollections of past lives. These experiences can provide clarity and healing, as they often reveal lessons learned or unresolved issues from previous incarnations. By tapping into the rich tapestry of the soul's journey, individuals can gain insights that resonate with their current life challenges and aspirations.

Journaling practices serve as a valuable complement to memory retrieval efforts. By writing down thoughts, feelings, and intuitive insights, individuals can create a tangible record of their spiritual experiences. Journaling can also facilitate the processing of emotions tied to past memories, allowing for deeper reflection and understanding. A dedicated journaling practice encourages individuals to explore recurring themes or symbols that may emerge, which can serve as clues to uncovering past life experiences. This written exploration can lead to profound realizations, as the act of writing often unlocks pathways to memories that may not surface during verbal reflection.

Meditation techniques specifically designed for accessing repressed memories can be transformative. Through focused meditation, practitioners can quiet the mind and cultivate a receptive state conducive to memory recall. Techniques such as body scanning or breath awareness can help individuals identify areas of tension or emotional blockages that may be linked to past experiences. By directing attention to these areas during meditation, one can invite memories to surface gently, allowing for a safe exploration of the past. This process can be enhanced through affirmations or mantras that reinforce the intention to uncover and heal past wounds.

Hypnotherapy is another effective method for accessing past lives and repressed memories. This therapeutic approach involves guiding individuals into a trance state where they can explore the depths of their subconscious mind. A trained hypnotherapist can help clients navigate their memories with sensitivity and care, ensuring that the process remains safe and supportive. As memories emerge, individuals can gain insights into their current life patterns and relationships, recognizing how past experiences influence their present. The therapeutic nature of hypnotherapy can facilitate profound healing and transformation, allowing individuals to integrate these insights into their daily lives and spiritual practices.

Integrating Spiritual Practices into Daily Life

Integrating spiritual practices into daily life can profoundly enhance the journey of self-discovery and memory recall. For those who believe in reincarnation and seek to explore the depths of their soul, the consistent application of spiritual techniques can be transformative. These practices create a sacred space where individuals can connect with their past lives, understand their current experiences, and foster a deeper connection to their spiritual essence. By incorporating meditation, journaling, and breathwork into everyday routines, practitioners can unlock the hidden memories that lie within, paving the way for profound insights and healing.

Meditation serves as a foundational practice in accessing repressed memories and past life experiences. Dedicating time each day to quiet the mind allows for greater clarity and focus. During these sessions, individuals can employ guided visualizations tailored to their specific intentions, such as recalling past life events or uncovering emotional blockages from previous incarnations.

By creating a tranquil environment and setting clear intentions, practitioners can facilitate deeper connections with their higher selves, ultimately enhancing their understanding of their spiritual journey.

Journaling is another powerful tool for memory retrieval and spiritual reflection. By documenting thoughts, feelings, and dreams, individuals can create a tangible record of their spiritual experiences, which can later serve as a reference for deeper analysis. This practice encourages self-exploration and provides an outlet for emotions that may surface during meditation or dream analysis. The act of writing can also spark memories that have been repressed, allowing individuals to explore their past lives more comprehensively and integrate those experiences into their current life.

Breathwork techniques offer an invaluable method for activating memories and facilitating emotional release. By using conscious breathing patterns, practitioners can access altered states of consciousness that facilitate memory recall. These techniques can be combined with other practices such as art therapy or guided visualization to deepen the experience. Engaging in breathwork not only enhances memory retrieval but also promotes relaxation and emotional balance, making it easier to confront and process past life memories that may evoke discomfort.

Participating in group workshops can further enrich the experience of integrating spiritual practices into daily life. Sharing the journey with others who have similar beliefs fosters a sense of community and support, enhancing the collective exploration of past lives. These workshops often incorporate various techniques such as hypnotherapy and Neuro-Linguistic Programming, allowing individuals to explore their memories in diverse and effective ways. The shared experiences and insights gained from group interactions can illuminate paths of understanding that may not have been accessible in solitary practice, ultimately leading to a more profound connection with one's spiritual identity.

13

Conclusion and Next Steps

Reflecting on the Journey of Memory Recall

Reflecting on the journey of memory recall invites a profound exploration of the layers of the self, particularly for those who embrace the beliefs surrounding reincarnation and the unseen dimensions of existence. Memory recall, especially in the context of past lives, requires a willingness to confront not only the experiences that shape our present but also those that may have been suppressed over time. This journey is often marked by a series of revelations that can be both enlightening and challenging, as individuals navigate the complexities of their inner landscapes. Understanding the mechanisms of memory recall—whether through guided visualization, meditation, or other techniques—becomes essential for those seeking to unlock the hidden narratives of their souls.

Guided visualization serves as a powerful tool for delving into past life memories, enabling practitioners to create a safe and supportive mental space. Through the use of imagery and focused intention, individuals can journey back to significant moments in their previous incarnations, uncovering insights that have been dormant. This technique not only enhances memory recall but also fosters a deeper connection to the spiritual aspects of one's existence. As participants engage with their past, they often find that these experiences resonate with their current life circumstances, providing clarity and understanding that can transform their present reality.

Journaling practices play a critical role in the memory retrieval process, serving as a bridge between the subconscious and conscious mind. Writing allows individuals to articulate their thoughts and feelings surrounding their experiences, often leading to unexpected breakthroughs. By documenting memories as they surface, practitioners can create a tapestry of their past, which can reveal patterns and themes that transcend lifetimes. Through this reflective process, the act of writing becomes a form of healing, facilitating the integration of past experiences into one's current narrative and empowering individuals to embrace their full spectrum of existence.

Meditation techniques, particularly those designed for accessing repressed memories, provide a pathway to deeper self-awareness and understanding. By quieting the mind and turning inward, practitioners can bypass the barriers that often prevent memory recall. This inward journey can be enhanced through breathwork, which not only calms the mind but also energizes the body, allowing for the release of stored emotions and memories. As individuals cultivate a meditative practice, they may uncover fragments of their past that illuminate their present, fostering a sense of continuity and purpose across lifetimes.

The collective aspect of memory recall is equally significant, as group workshops offer a space for shared exploration and connection. Engaging with others on similar journeys can amplify personal insights and foster a sense of community. Techniques such as neuro-linguistic programming and art therapy can further enrich these experiences, enabling participants to access and express memories in diverse ways. As believers in reincarnation and spiritual exploration come together, they create a supportive environment that not only enhances individual recall but also nurtures a collective understanding of the interconnectedness of all souls, paving the way for profound healing and transformation.

Continuing the Exploration of the Soul

Continuing the exploration of the soul requires a multifaceted approach that acknowledges the complexity of human experience and the myriad ways in which memory can be accessed and understood. For believers in reincarnation and spiritualists, the journey into past lives is often a deeply personal and transformative experience. By employing memory recall techniques, individuals can unlock repressed experiences that may hold the key to understanding their current life circumstances. Practices such as guided visualization can serve as powerful tools in this exploration, allowing individuals to navigate the recesses of their minds and reconnect with memories that may have been long buried.

Guided visualization serves not only as a method for recollection but also as a means of creating a safe space for exploration. Practitioners can lead individuals through a series of mental exercises that promote relaxation and focus, facilitating access to past life memories. This technique, when combined with journaling practices, can enhance the recall process. Journaling provides an outlet for individuals to document their experiences, thoughts, and emotions, creating a tangible record that can be revisited and analyzed. This documentation not only aids memory retrieval but also fosters a deeper understanding of the connections between past and present.

Meditation techniques play a crucial role in accessing repressed memories. By calming the mind and tuning into the inner self, individuals can create an environment conducive to uncovering hidden truths. Regular meditation practice can enhance one's sensitivity to subtle memories, allowing for a more profound connection with the past. In conjunction with hypnotherapy, which can induce a trance-like state conducive to memory access, these practices can open gateways to experiences that have shaped the soul's journey across lifetimes.

Art therapy provides another avenue for exploration, enabling individuals to express their repressed experiences in creative forms. Engaging in artistic activities can bypass the analytical mind, allowing the subconscious to surface memories that might otherwise remain inaccessible.

This form of therapy can be particularly beneficial for those who find it challenging to articulate their experiences verbally. Combining art therapy with breathwork can further enhance memory activation, as the conscious act of breathing deeply can facilitate emotional release and clarity, aiding in the retrieval of past life insights.

Lastly, group workshops for shared memory exploration foster a sense of community and support. These gatherings create an environment where individuals can share their experiences and insights, leading to collective healing and understanding. Incorporating techniques from neurolinguistic programming can also enhance memory recall, providing participants with the tools to reframe their narratives and deepen their understanding of their soul's journey. Spiritual practices, such as rituals and guided meditations, can further assist in uncovering hidden memories, creating a holistic approach to the ongoing exploration of the soul.

Resources for Further Learning and Practice

For those seeking to delve deeper into memory recall techniques and the exploration of repressed experiences, a wealth of resources is available to enhance your journey. Books and online courses focusing on memory retrieval can provide foundational knowledge and practical exercises. Authors such as Brian Weiss and Michael Newton offer insights into past life regression and the therapeutic aspects of memory work. Their writings often include case studies and techniques that can serve as a guide for personal exploration. Additionally, engaging with platforms like Udemy or Coursera can introduce structured learning pathways that align with your interests in spiritual practices and memory recall.

Guided visualization is a powerful tool for accessing past life memories, and various resources can assist in mastering this technique. Numerous audio recordings and apps are dedicated to guided meditations specifically designed for past life exploration. Listening to expert practitioners can help you visualize and uncover hidden experiences, facilitating a deeper connection to your subconscious. Furthermore, workshops led by experienced guides often combine visualization with other techniques, providing a holistic approach to memory recall that can enrich your understanding and practice.

Journaling serves as a vital practice for memory retrieval, and a range of resources can help cultivate this skill. Books on expressive writing and memory journaling can offer prompts and exercises designed to unlock suppressed memories and encourage self-reflection. Online communities and forums also provide a space for sharing experiences and insights, fostering a sense of connection with others on similar journeys. Incorporating journaling into your daily routine can yield significant benefits, allowing for a structured way to document revelations and patterns that emerge over time.

Meditation techniques tailored for repressed memories can enhance your ability to access deeper layers of consciousness. Various guided meditation resources are available, including apps like Insight Timer and Headspace, which provide sessions focused on memory activation and healing. Additionally, joining meditation circles or groups that focus on spiritual growth can create an environment conducive to collective exploration. These practices not only enhance personal experiences but also cultivate a greater sense of community among those exploring similar themes.

Finally, consider exploring the therapeutic potential of hypnotherapy and art therapy for uncovering repressed experiences. Many trained professionals offer workshops and individual sessions that combine these modalities, allowing for a safe space to explore past life memories creatively. Art therapy, in particular, can help express emotions and insights that may be difficult to articulate verbally. Breathwork and dream analysis are also valuable practices to integrate into your exploration, as they can reveal significant insights into your past. Engaging with these resources can open new pathways to understanding your soul's journey and enrich your spiritual practice.

www.ingramcontent.com/pod-product-compliance
Lightning Source LLC
LaVergne TN
LVHW022227200926
848481LV00006B/2162
* 9 7 9 8 3 4 8 5 7 0 0 0 2 *